Watching the Weather

Snow

Elizabeth Miles

Heinemann Library
Chicago, Illinois

Customer Service 888-454-2279
Visit our website at www.heinemannlibrary.com

Designed by Richard Parker and Q2A Solutions
Illustrations: Jeff Edwards
Originated by Dot Gradations Ltd.
Printed and bound in China by South China Printing
Company

09 08 07 06 05
10 9 8 7 6 5 4 3 2 1

**Library of Congress Cataloging-in-Publication
Data**
Miles, Elizabeth, 1960-
    Snow / Elizabeth Miles.
        p. cm. -- (Watching the weather)
    Includes bibliographical references and index.
    ISBN 1-4034-6551-7 -- ISBN 1-4034-6556-8 (pbk.)
1. Snow--Juvenile literature. I. Title. II. Series.
QC926.37.M55 2005
551.57'84--dc22
                            2004018486

Acknowledgments
The Publishers would like to thank the following for
permission to reproduce photographs: Alamy pp. 12
(Bryan & Cherry Alexander), 20 (David Sanger), 21
(Chris Fredriksson); Corbis pp. 4 (Jose Luis Pelaez, Inc.),
5, 9 (Ariel Skelley), 16 (Tom Brakefield), 22 (Reuters),
24; FLPA p. 26; Getty Images pp. 7 (PhotoDisc), 8
(Taxi/Anne-Marie Webber), 10 (PhotoDisc), 13 (Image
Bank/Kirk Anderson), 14 (Stone/John Marshall), 15
(Image Bank/Alan Majchrowicz), 17 (Stone/Daniel J.
Cox), 18 (Image Bank/Mike Brinson); Reuters p. 23
(Paul Darrow); Science Photo Library p.25 (Mauro
Fermariello); Still Pictures p. 27 (A. Riedmiller); Topham
Picturepoint pp. 11 (Kent Meireis/The Image Works),
19; Tudor Photography pp. 28, 29.

Cover photograph of trees covered in snow in
Washington, USA, reproduced with permission of Getty
Images/The Image Bank.

The Publishers would like to thank Daniel Ogden for
his assistance in the preparation of this book.

Every effort has been made to contact copyright
holders of any material reproduced in this book. Any
omissions will be rectified in subsequent printings if
notice is given to the Publisher.

Contents

Some words are shown in bold, **like this**. You can find out what they mean by looking in the glossary.

What Is Snow?

Snow is ice that falls from the sky in the form of snowflakes. Lots of fallen snowflakes can cover the ground and other surfaces outside.

A covering of snow can make everything look white.

Some people use sleds to ride over the snow.

After a snowfall, the snow can **melt** or stay in a layer on the ground. Sometimes the snow stays and another snowfall makes the snow thicker.

Where Does Snow Come From?

Snow is made up of tiny pieces of ice called **ice crystals**. The ice crystals form from **water vapor** in cold clouds.

Snowflakes are six-sided shapes made of ice crystals.

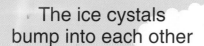The ice cystals
bump into each other

The ice crystals
make snowflakes

Water in the air
(water vapor)
freezes into ice crystals

As the water in the air **freezes**, ice
crystals bump into each other and stick
together to make snowflakes. Every
snowflake looks different.

Snowflakes

Snowflakes can be small or large, hard or soft. Snowflakes often **melt** on their way down from the clouds and reach the ground as raindrops.

Large snowflakes can be made up of hundreds of **ice crystals**.

Small snowflakes can be very powdery and may not stick together.

Small, hard snowflakes can sting your face in the wind. Large, soft snowflakes look fluffy. Some snowflakes stick together easily so you can make snowmen or snowballs.

When Does It Snow?

Snow usually falls in winter. In the winter, the air and ground are often very cold. Fallen snow stays frozen while it is cold and **melts** when it gets warmer.

Skiing on snow is a popular sport in the winter.

When fallen snow melts, it changes. First, it melts into **slush**, and then water. Then it drains away or dries up. This can take a few days or several weeks.

In the summer, the snow melts and people enjoy walking and bicycling instead of skiing.

Snow Around the World

Places such as hot deserts and the **tropical regions** have no snow all year. The weather is too hot for snow. Other places have snowfalls throughout the year.

In the cold **Arctic**, snow covers the ground for most of the year.

As you climb a high mountain, it often gets colder. Near the top there may be snow.

The tops of mountains can have snow all year long. This is because the air is very cold high up. The place where this snow starts is called the snowline.

Snow and Plants

Some plants grow and flower in the winter snow. A layer of snow can be like a blanket. It covers plants and keeps them warm.

These winter flowers are called snowdrops.

Fir trees grow on mountain slopes where there is lots of snow. Layers of snow can be heavy and can break tree branches. Fir trees have a special shape so this does not happen.

Heavy snow will slide off the sloping branches of fir trees.

Snow and Animals

Some animals live in places where there is lots of snow. The snowshoe hare has large, furry paws for hopping across the snow.

The snowshoe hare's big feet stop it from sinking into soft, deep snow.

The Arctic fox's white coat is difficult to see against the white snow.

The Arctic fox's brown coat turns white in winter. This means that **predators** cannot see it easily. Its winter fur is woolly and warm, too.

Snow and People

Snow can be fun. As more snow falls, the heavy weight packs it down firmly. This firm snow is good for skiing, snowboarding, and other sports.

Snowboarders can slide very fast on firm snow.

Some people wear snowshoes to stop them from sinking into deep snow.

It is important to stay warm in snowy weather. People wear warm clothes and keep moving around while they are outside in the cold.

Staying Safe

Snowy weather can be dangerous. When bright sunlight **reflects** off the snow, it can hurt our eyes. It is important to wear sunglasses.

Mountain climbers wear sunglasses to protect their eyes from sunshine reflecting off the snow.

Driving too fast during a snowfall can cause an accident. Cars can slide on snowy streets. Sometimes car wheels get stuck in thick snow.

Some people put chains on their car wheels. These help grip the snow.

Snowstorms

A **blizzard** is a winter snowstorm. Strong winds blow and lots of snow falls quickly. It is difficult to see anything in a blizzard.

Snow ploughs try to keep main roads clear during blizzards.

The wind may blow the falling snow into piles called **snowdrifts**. Snowdrifts can cover cars and trains so that the people inside have to be rescued.

A snowdrift can be as high as a house.

Disaster: Avalanche

An avalanche is when a lot of snow suddenly slides down a mountainside. Lots of things can cause an avalanche, such as a thick layer of new snow.

An avalanche can fall down a mountainside in a few seconds.

Trained dogs use their sense of smell to find people buried in an avalanche.

The heavy snow in an avalanche can damage houses. It can bury people or even whole villages. There is little warning, so people cannot always get away.

Is It Snow?

An icy white covering might be **frost** and not snow. Frost does not fall from clouds as snowflakes. It forms from **water vapor** in the air close to the ground.

Frost can cover the ground and objects outside. It can look just like snow.

Fake snow is sometimes sprayed on ski slopes if no real snow has fallen.

Sometimes people make fake snow. It is used to film winter scenes in movies and on television. Pretend snow can be made from ice, paper, plastic, or **chemicals**.

Project: How to Measure Snow

Now that you know how snow is made, you can find out how much frozen water there is in snow.

You will need:
- a straight-sided glass jar
- a ruler
- cardboard
- snow

1. Find a flat layer of snow outside and measure its depth with a ruler.

2. Hold the jar upside-down. Push it down through the snow into the ground.

3. Slide the cardboard underneath so that you gather the snow in the jar.

4. Let the snow in the jar **melt**. Measure the depth of the water left in the jar.

5. Compare the snow measurement with the water measurement.

Why is the snow deeper than the melted water? It is because there is lots of air trapped in the snow, making it thicker.

Glossary

Arctic very cold area near the North Pole

blizzard snowstorm with strong winds

chemical substance used by scientists to make all kinds of things, such as medicine

freeze turn into a very cold solid (water freezes into ice)

frost frozen water vapor close to the ground

ice crystal very tiny amount of frozen water

melt change from a solid to a liquid (ice melts into water)

predator animal that hunts another animal for food

reflects bounces off

slush mix of ice and water

snowdrift thick snow that piles up in the wind

snow plough machine with big blades for pushing thick snow off roads

tropical region part of Earth where the weather is hot and wet

water vapor water in the air. Water vapor is a gas that we cannot see.

More Books to Read

Ashwell, Miranda, and Owen, Andy. *What is Weather?: Snow*. Chicago: Heinemann Library, 2002.

Bundey, Nikki. *Science of Weather: Snow and the Earth*. Minneapolis: Carolrhoda Books, 2001.

Butterfield, Moira. *Looking at Animals in Cold Places*. Chicago: Raintree, 2000.

Index